Dried Flowers

Dried Flowers

by
Fred Cogswell

Borealis Press Ltd.
Ottawa, Canada
2002

Copyright © by Fred Cogswell
and Borealis Press Ltd., 2002

*All rights reserved. No part of this book may
be used or reproduced in any manner whatsoever without
written permission except in the case of brief quotations
embodied in critical articles and reviews.*

Canada

*The Publishers acknowledge the financial assistance
of the Government of Canada through the Book Publishing
Industry Development Program (BPIDP)
for our publishing activities*

National Library of Canada Cataloguing in Publication Data

Cogswell, Fred, 1917-
   Dried Flowers

Poems.
ISBN 0-88887-208-9

   I. Title.

PS8555.O3D75 2002   C811'.54   C2002-900916-2
PR9199.3.C64D75 2002

Cover design by Bull's Eye Design, Ottawa
Typesetting by Chisholm Communications, Ottawa

Printed and bound in Canada on acid-free paper

Contents

To Tongue's Surprise 1
What Can I Write You? What Can I Say? 2
Wild Fancies 4
An Aper 6
Without A Tune 8
When The Doctor Gave Me A Pill 10
The World From Galaxy To Worm 12
When I Visit 14
A Large Charity With A Religious Twist 16
Circumstance 18
Although 20
Despoiling 21
The Crucifix 23
The White Duck 29
Bather 31
By Way Of A Will 32
Why It Is Not The Same 34
The Sacrifice 35
Snow And Nostalgia 36
Unfulfilled Dreams 37
October 39
The Life I Lived 41
For Adele 43
Haikus 44
Reality 48
The Poet 49
In Songs We Love 52
As If 54
The Little Church 56
Poet 57
We Must Play Well 58
After Beowulf 59
The Crows 64

Glooms 65
This Day 66
Nocturne 68
Wounds 70
Time's Bright Ash And The Small Dust Of Daylight . . . 71
Energism 72
Song 73
An Old Story 74
The Robin In The Woods 75
Common Denominator 76
One Of Life's First Allegories 77
Meeting 78
Suffering Is Not 79
Life 80
An Autumn Conceit 81
Roles 82
After A Wasp-Bite 83
An Impasse 84
L'envoi 85
Professor 86
Pot-Pourri 87
Shadows 88
As Time Runs Itself 89
The Willow Basket 90
There Were Two Of Them 91
A Sail Has Dreamed 92
Metaphysical 93
The Lament Of Cresseid 94
Last Verse 98
Letter To A Young Poet 99
Final Song 100
The Young Tarentine 102
Soil 104
Of All The Words 106
O Night Among All Nights 107

Foreword

Dried Flowers is in all that it stands for a labour of love. Two thirds of the text was typed out by my wife, Adele Cogswell, before her ultimately fatal illness put an ending to such work. I had recourse as volunteers: to her daughter Sarah Bartlett and to Lawrence Hutchman, head of the Writer's Federation of New Brunswick. Finally I asked Roger Ploude for help and got it in five minutes. I am very grateful for Roger and for Vera Zarowsky who finished the necessary typing. All the same, *Dried Flowers* belonged to Adele as it belonged to no-one else. If proof is required it can be contained in two quotations. The proof of love is contained in my poem, "The Water and the Rock".

> Hard rock was I, and she was water flowing,
> Over sharp stones of opposition going;
> Shaping herself to me as to a cup.
>
> She filled the valleys of my ego up
> With a cool, smooth compliance everywhere
> As yielding and unhurtable as air.
>
> Soft was my love as water, and I forgot
> In the calm wash of compliant rhythm caught,
> How water shapes and softens, sculpts and smooths
> The channel of the rock through which it moves.

That love can be tempered with justice and the courage that faces convention is in Adele's case covered by the authorities of Saint Thomas University who on the 28th January, 2002, conferred the degree of Bachelor of Arts, posthumously upon her, a degree as deserved as it is rare in its bestowal.

Fred Cogswell
January, 2002

To Tongue's Surprise

To tongue's surprise no taste is ever dumb.
It can't withstand the leaf's willow-dapple.
Nor the rich barbed thrust of crab-apple.
Wild taste offers unexpected freedom.

From comb-clogged wax I feel strong honey come.
The mild ripe seed of caraway caressed
My mouth as dry as a late Fall harvest,
My jaws made a good chew out of spruce gum.

Tang of tansey and cool mint. Such things blend
To build a rare, inexplicable end
Where two extremes meet enough to be real
As they return to justify impulse:
One is cold water in raw oatmeal;
The other, purple-salt-royale called dulse.

What Can I Write You? What Can I Say?

What can I write to you? What can I say?
The times to talk and act come often now.
Though passion's past and we enjoy the day
Night's love is gone and with it went the glow.
Our adult joys were wonderful to know
But though our worlds are soft and we are free
Life's still twin-selves still fuse, dissolve, and flow,
Bathing the sense in plural ecstasy

What can I write to you? What can I say?
Talk and action are things we should forego
When young love finds that each gets in the way
Of both who in separate selves have no
Need for anything to make being flow
To oneness except for propinquity
Whose fusion we had hoped would never go,
Leaving solitude with no ecstasy.

What can I write to you? What can I say?
It's not from high to high that great lives flow.
Twilight can be in place for every day
So much we are given when lights are low
And circumstance claims that all things are so.
Some lives there are, though, that mean more than be
And help each of our egos to pull through
At the low cost of faded ecstasy.

For most, life offers a varied load
To suit the demands of a varied day,
But when it happens that beings explode
To be one, cry "Peace, get out of the way!"

Wild Fancies

In a sky harsh as garnet
black birds in a gliding flow
drop down a bloody sunset
with strange shapes I do not know,
and their stillness is a blow
to all who attend to life.
Now everywhere they go
their colour cuts like a knife.

A tinge abandons velvet
and leads a dirtier flow
in air where a few beams yet
attempt a half-healthy glow
but vanish where all birds go
out of dreams and out of life.
Now like words as pure as snow
such darkness cuts like a knife.

I see the white and regret
the black as the yes and no
of contrast here have upset
my years with how matters go
toward an end I do not know.
How can offices in strife
be done with the ebb and flow
and bring unity of life.

Sweet Prince, I shall not forget
what future has now begun.
Can coda and staccatto
Find peace and strife are but one?

An Aper

An aper of adult conduct
When I was little and afraid
I was compelled to reconstruct
A self whose likeness when displayed
Was not what its appearance said.
Observant but without a thought,
I took on roles I never played
With no real knowledge of the plot.

An aper of absurd conduct
I learned to trade acts for words, pare
These to a logical construct
And in all instances find there
Excitement that will wear and wear....
A consistency that will not
Be bought or sold but everywhere
Will bring meaning to each fresh spot.

An aper of adult conduct
I follow now, quite unafraid,
The plays that ideas construct,
Whether I fill or lack or trade
Games are more than the mess we made:
Underneath time and space in thought,
Though shapes may change and details fade
Challenges ripen with our lot.

Come, good Prince, whether gold or dross,
Offer your hardest dreams to me;
Out of a paradise of loss
We learn that mean is more than be.

Without A Tune

Now that the world, a tangle of all green
Shades, lets invisible sap, wild with sun,
Write form and colour on all that had been
White and grey; listen to the melt begun
Of ancient ice celebrating its run
Of frenzy under lifeless sun and moon
That have no meaning and, lacking one,
Cannot from my acts create any tune.

The shape and lure of things can only mean
Life-music as time makes our feelings run
Through interlacing beams and what has been
Is reinforced by hearing one by one
Recurring beats that gild the occasion.
I have no envy for the sun and moon;
Despite energy by which they run.
No life is possible without a tune.

The tune that builds for me a living scene
And kills it after all my acts are gone
Exists through memory, its only mean
The consciousness that we have done what's done:
True existence is grass upon the lawn
That seeds and grows and dies and, late or soon,
In context with all others then is gone.
No life's possible without sun and moon.

Thank God, great Prince! No part we play is mean.
Complex in scale means more than sun or moon.
Let us rejoice inside each changing scene.
No life is possible without a tune.

When The Doctor Gave Me A Pill

When the doctor gave me a pill
I did not find its flavour sweet
It told me that he thinks I still
Have an irregular heart-beat
Though rest might make the cure complete.
This opinion I must decline.
No "might be" future can compete
With all today's "now" which still is mine

This chance to be a doctor's shill
Marked my gambling career's defeat.
It told me better than a pill
Was squander "now" and not retreat
To "maybe". The one great deceit
Life can't bear is to fit in line
Time's measurements and delete
Difference between "yours" and "mine".

The truth is, measurements don't kill
They are only there to repeat
Location. What lies beyond their skill
Are expectations packaged neat
And only limited by "complete"
That try to put in a straight line
Energy's individual beat
Whose form no symbols can align.

When the doctor gave me his pill
It gave two choices to betray:
I have some faith in another's skill
But my great I am blurs the way.

The World From Galaxy To Worm

The world from galaxy to worm
Is using up its energy,
Changing its shapes from form to form
Is more than mere viscosity.
Whatever states one's senses see,
By long use concentrated on,
Can subsume the mass and be
Our only truth until it's gone.

The world from galaxy, to worm
Is wide in its variety.
It changes shape, turns uniform
To put what seems reality
In place of all we cannot see?
Inside us where our lives are drawn
We know paradoxically
A world that never was its own.

The world from galaxy to worm
Substitutes *do* for *be*,
But what is done is never firm
Enough to make us all agree
On what life is or death may be,
Having but faith to rely on
But void of vision's certainty
What use were his eyes to Samson?

The world from galaxy to worm?
It's best, sweet Prince, we don't agree
With time to spend in seeking form
And no responsibility.

When I Visit

When I visit, after a year's disguise,
The farmer whose area was my country
What I remember is blurred by new eyes
This place has become subtly strange to me
And the more I call upon memory
The more the one I know is forced to find
How much all that has happened to be
Works in its own way only in its mind.

When I visit, although family ties
Seem to cement a lengthy history
What part of part of them is truth and what part lies
Depends on each one's innate mystery.
But who sorts out idiosyncrasy?
Therefore to use what cannot be defined
Each one must catch his own veracity
That comes and grows through crannies of the mind.

When I visit, an impulse in me tries
To answer questions that I cannot see
And form conclusions that a mind might prize
By measurements that more or less agree.
To find support in uniformity
Is part of all the academic grind
Where our eyes write "contemporary"
To please shallow establishments of mind.

Good Prince! I am not one of those that dies
Although a cause can unify the mind
And bring new colour to its skies;
All measurement is limited or blind.

A Large Charity With A Righteous Twist...

A large charity with a righteous twist
Asks for money to feed Afghanistan
Ravaged by force that no one could resist
As new weapons put down the Taliban.
Now a new breed unveils its battle plan
And calls itself a legal government
Sanctified by the snobbishness of man
That disguises power to fit a fresh intent.

Winter comes. Money's needed and money's missed—
An urgency lies in Afghanistan
Too strong for charity to resist.
What's needed now is human greed whose span
Is state guaranteed investment. No ban
On income-tax donations whose per cent
Of profit is so large that any man
Might wonder what such gross bribery meant.

Now to get one's name on such a list?
What permanent belief can make a man?
How tell any one from a terrorist?
In what sense can one hope or fear or plan.
Can one fix colour where all colours ran?
What do computers know of government
More than it's U.S. or Afghan?
Ask of event now where the money went.

Great Prince! It is not easy to resist
The world that compels us or to let it go.
Let the world you have grind an honest grist
And confess all the things you do not know.

Circumstance

Each circumstance that makes our minds perform
Affects our fingers in the ways we play
And will never carry out any norm
As exactly as printed notes convey.

Everywhere around me, deeper than speech,
World-circumstance becomes world-energy
In feelings unrepressed whose powers reach
A massive serendipity.

Its mystery is stronger than mystique….
Years ago at luncheon I met one day
A U.S. pianist, John Kirkpatrick,
Whom I'd heard of but never had heard play.

He was a thin, small man, a dandy who
Prated old ideas, their truths long gone,
And he acted like a lady's man, too,
As he talked music to my companion.

But I let these things pass. This man was great,
Worth all the respect of every one.
In one performance and upon one date
He did what no one else had ever done.

Nineteen-thirty-nine, at Carnegie Hall....
His playing made Ives' "Concorde Sonata" whole.
In a miracle magical to all
He clothed a banker's music with a soul.

Although

Although the singer's voice was sweet and strong
And the simple air fuelled feeling's key
The lyrist's words in their brass honesty
Brought richer life to the lilt of song.

Despoiling
After the French of Eddy Boudreau (1914-1954)

November had begun its work,
A task of despoiling.
I have just heard the sobbing countryside....
Anxious about Winter's preludes
It shuddered beyond control.
I noticed thousands of things going to perish....
Nature was sad,
God-like trees mourning beauty!
Tall trees with different shapes
Without colour, without leaves, without birds!
After upholding a dream they cried from nostalgia;
After having lodged trilling birds
They seem infinitely alone!
Oh! A few yellowed, withered leaves
Crazy from a storm
Clung to them like pledges of loyalty
Where a short time ago
A home in birches has been exalted.

We drove by and the scenery disappeared.
Behind us, however
It returned to dust
–An omen for the end of mankind.

What an image, what a likeness!
What splendour in this period of collapse!
Autumn, grandeur, and decrepitude!

I have heard differing noises....
Above all the cry of breeze-petrified branches
I looked at rust-coloured fields.
I saw men tear the earth apart
And this ending pierced my soul....
I thought I saw there
All of humanity's suffering.

The Crucifix

After the French of Alphonse de Lamertine

To you who from her dying mouth gave me
Both the latest breath she had and her last adieu,
Two sacred symbols, a gift from one who ceased to be
    And God's own image too.

How the tears spilled on your feet an adoring balm
After the holy hour when you, about to die,
Into my trembling hands transferred, alive and warm,
    Your love from love's last sigh.

Holy torches have thrown one last flame that still lives,
The priest murmured dirges that were sweet and mild
Like the lullabies a murmuring woman gives
    To soothe her sleeping child.

Within her pious brow pure hope preserved its trace
And on her features, struck by an August beauty,
The doleful fugitive had imprinted the grace
    Of death's great majesty.

The wind caressing her dishevelled hair was dumb
Yet violated the truth that it wished to show
As we can see float on a white mausoleum
   A black cypress shadow.

One of her arms hung down from the dark bed of death
And violated the truth it wanted to share
Still seeming to look and press on her mouth the breath
   And face of her saviour.

Her lips were partly open like a loving cup,
But her soul in that divine kiss left no trace,
Like a light perfume which a flame eats up
   Before its last embrace.

Now all things slept. Her icy mouth sheer cold expressed
Inside her sleeping breast her struggling breath was stilled
And carelessly in her eyes were the lids depressed;
   She was indeed half-killed.

And I, standing, in the death grip of terror caught
Did not dare to go near her admired resting place
As if by such trespass mute majesty could not
   Be consecrated grace.

I did not dare! ... but the priest could my sadness see
And the crucifix from her frozen fingers took:
"Behold here hope and behold here memory.
   Keep both of them unstuck."

Yes, you'll stay with me, funereal heritage,
Seven times since the day when I planted the tree
On her nameless tomb, it has changed all its leafage.
   You are not gone from me.

Placed near the heart, alas! Where all things their
   worlds efface,
You are, against time, forbidden your memory
and drop by drop my eyes have implanted their trace
   Upon soft ivory.

O lost confidant of the soul that flew by choice,
Come, rest on my heart! Speak now and tell me true
What is she saying here as her enfeebled voice
    No longer reaches you.

At that doubtful hour when the soul seems dead
Hiding itself under veils drawn over our eyes,
Outside of our feeling, step by step recharted,
    Are clearly two last good-byes.

When between life and the uncertainties of death
Like a fruit by its own weight detached from its bough
Our soul is suspended and trembles at each breath,
    Open the tomb right now.

When all the songs and sobs of confused harmony
Will no longer let the sleepy spirit peace attend,
On the lips of the dying, glued in ecstacy
    May be found one last friend.

To light the horror of this narrow passage
To raise up to God all His disgruntled gaze
Divine Consoler for when we kiss the image,
    Answer, "What is it he says?"

You know, know how to die! And weep divinely
In this terrible night when prayers are forlorn;
For the holy olive here soaks its roots finely
    From evening to morn

From the cross where your eye knew mystery's birth
You saw your mother in tears and all nature doomed!
Like us you left your friend behind on the earth
    With your body entombed!

In the name of that death may my weakness obtain
In relief from your breathing that dolorous sigh;
When my hour comes, you will remember again.
    You who knew how to die!

I shall search for the past where her expiring mouth
Exhaled on my feet irrecoverable farewell
And her soul will guard my soul back to the truth,
   To God's bosom as well.

It may be when on my funeral bed I lie
Like a weeping angel, at once both calm and sage,
A mourning figure will then to my mouth apply
   The boldest heritage!

Uphold her last footsteps and make firm her last will,
and let consecrate pledges of hope and love burn
So that she who has died and she who lives still
   Will be one at each turn

Until the day when dead men pierce the sombre tomb
And, calling seven times up in the sky, their loss
Together will waken those who sleep in the gloom
   Of the eternal cross!

THE WHITE DUCK
After the French of Rina Lasnier

He aimed at black and killed the white
If you shatter its wings upon your pond's hard ice
And carefully plan to use Winter-bread when you throw
Or make it bleed; trapped in the cold singer's voice
The dream's white shadow will fade from the very snow.

O my Prince, how wicked you are!
Under its song it bleeds away.

In vain do you melt snow to forget your victim
—Snow that in space expands to erase smiles and frowns—
Do you stare at the bird to scatter its white plumes again?
Your heart still rolls in a tumult of hunting and hounds.

O my Prince! How wicked you are!
All its feathers gone in the wind.

On swift-flying air, shadow and wind tanned your
  dream,
But the wing held onto your wake in the light.
Each time red blood for this trip the bird will redeem.
Pick it up then from the depths, think on your
  hands' weight.

O my Prince! How wicked you are!
Aimed at black and killed the white.

Bather

After the French of Saint-Denys-Garneau (1912-1943)

Ah! Morning on the sea, and in my eyes
A sun-lit bather has gathered to herself
All the light of the landscape

By Way Of A Will
After the French of Pierre Trottier

Every day that I see I capture from death
Every poem that I write I draw from a dead man

If I have any virtue it shines in my sin
My candle is shadow and my flame is the moment

If my body is wax that is burnt by my love
My life is a night that devours my days

In me all things are sad to be riddled with laughter
And when I die there is nothing

More to take from me perhaps than the grey bones
Of colourless silence that will leave me to smile

For the alarms and rumours which I have spread
And for the poem that death will write on my features

For the definitive addiction of my soul
I confess this poem to the eternal embalmer
For the definitive edition of my soul.

While for my body's printing I would like a few
Old verses from the good earth of my flesh

These are the only things in which I endeavour to match
For my pleasure the dead in whose house resounds

The most perfect measure of a final sigh.

Why It Is Not The Same

There are no clouds today. Sun-rays have hurled
Their beams so bright the dew has left the lawn.
Here is pure air enough to feed the world
But she who breathed with me as one is gone.

The Sacrifice

After the French of Leconte de Lisle

Immortal Liqueur, under Heaven, nothing's worth more.
The blessed blood, the triumphal blood, that blood-
    burst
Love spurts from the heart in living streams that pour
To staunch our still unassuageable thirst.

Far up, in the awesome height of freedom's air
Man and his Gods wished to be closer than allowed;
The bleeding holocaust smoked upon the stake there
And its odour rose toward an implacable cloud.

Taming the flesh, atremble with its rebellions,
Offering God death as expiatory deed,
The martyr has lain down under the teeth of lions
In royal purple as upon a glory bed.

But the bitter delight in suffering never dies.
If heaven is empty and the Gods are no more
I would love, although my heart was spoiled in His eyes,
To bathe with my blood Divinity I adore.

Snow And Nostalgia
After the French of Simone Routier

You fall, snow, again and again on broken soil, then
    tender and meek,
On my country's uncomplaining earth; playfully,
    sportively,
    you fall
From my country where I have left my footsteps
    certain springs
    behind,
Where I have left without coming back to see
    whether it was
    still there,
Whether it was still sturdy and cruel and tumultuous
    and intact,
You fall, O snow, thick, straight down, in circles, my
    country's snow,
You fall obstinately, upon yourself, tirelessly
You fall, in eddies that blind, pillage and disable.
In eddies you fall, distraught and deadly
You fall down there on my country,
And I am not in it.

UNFULFILLED DREAMS

After the French of Guy Arsenault

The father has lived for the son, putting upon him
the illusory hope of everything he had not been....

So from generation to generation, from branch to branch
are transmitted the unfulfilled dreams of ancestors.

The fiddling of all cowardly individuals ... bitternesses
that snowball when the son become father looks
at his own world with the same three centuries
old spectacles

So many family trees are straggling spruce; they
heap up mountains without ever touching the stars....

The most beautiful tree in the mountain
has been struck by thunder.

A fiery zigzag
tearing heaven in two
has reached it from head to roots

Two long beams of blackened wood
have fallen again as every
tall thing falls; with a racket.

The summits attract powder
Beauty has its price
Greatness is held in balance
from powder kegs to guns.

OCTOBER

After Bliss Carman

With a hood of purple berries
And a cloak of gay attire
Comes the gypsy maid October
To set the hills on fire.

She's a kiss of scarlet colours
On a mouth that sumac dyes,
And her frosty touch is magic
To the blue of Autumn skies;

For it tempts with tang of clear days
An Earth grown drab and old
To have one fling at living
Ere Winter come and cold.

So the green turns gold in burning
Or flaunts in orange fire
Where the dying leaves determine
To have a splendid pyre.

And though you fly no banners
Nor blazon bright in view,
The gypsy maid, October,
Will work her will on you.

With a breath of vine-sweet fragrance
And a wisp of early frost,
She will tease your tired senses
Till their jadedness is lost.

She will charm your heart from boredom
With her vivid reckless mood
Till the old mad zest of being
Goes coursing through your blood....

In days of listless languor
When the cyder apples fall
Comes the gypsy maid, October,
To break the Summer's thrall.

The Life I Lived…

The life I lived need not have been the same
As it has seemed to those who know me best.
It's not to me that I owe my good name.

Somewhere in my genes beyond praise or blame
Was potential. Chance and time did the rest.
The life I lived need not have been the same

And would not have been so had but my name
Been different, and other parents pressed.
It's not to me that I owe my good name

Who, at the right time when the right chance came,
Took it, and floated to the future's crest.
The life I lived need not have been the same

Had other things come to me, but in the game
Of life what occurred occurred unguessed.
It's not to me that I owe my good name.

Who knows potential enough to proclaim
Whether in my self I was cursed or blessed?
The life I lived need not have been the same;
It's not to me that I owe my good name.

For Adele

              For you I put
With my left hand,
The sacred tobacco
Into the rising flame.

Its taste is hot and sweet

HAIKUS

After the French of Jocelyne Villeneuve

The End of Night
A new day rises
gently; it makes light pregnant
with remembered stars.

Sunrise
While rubbing her paws
the fussy fly is lighting
rays of gold flame.

In the Woods
Paganini....
The frail-leafed fern brandishes
its violins.

Gymnast
Grasshopper meadows,
rose and yellow and green, see,
the grass is bouncing.

Road Companion
While hiking in June …
A butterfly preceded me,
stops … then waits for me.

Story of the Heart
The highs and the lows–
like the fountain's water-jets
Life has ups and downs.

The Owl
It is dark. An owl
inside its sunflower-eyes
has discerned the day.

Invocation
A disturbing night.…
The osprey's piercing cry is
recalling a storm.

Correspondence
The wind-blown flowers
tremble in nervous meadows–
Summer's here at last.

Tortoise
is not a stone
is not rewarmed in sunshine–
It moves.

Uncertainty
Come-and-go of thought–
the willows waver over
what should be their turn.

Snob
The humming-bird
flies by here and flies by there
without seeing me.

Quarrel
The words fall heavy….
Rain is beating on the roof–
Ultimate rage.

Lovers Beneath the Rain
Hand in hand they go–
Gold threads tying together
Both earth and heaven.

Irony
Colours of summer
Mixed with the cries of a child
who is not my own.

Destiny
They talk of flowers
I have not seen and Summer
that will come no more.

REALITY

After the French of Andrée Chaurette

There will be that pain
For breaking
Tomorrow
In broad daylight

And the wall for scaling
And that old worm-eaten door
For breaking down

And our images will tremble
As they touch the material
That disappoints and thrills
And our eyes will sparkle
At the unsupportable radiance
Of that unlooked for light.

The Poet: 1
After the French of Calixte Duguay

In the wasteland the poet fares
While the hunter goes on a spree
He swaggers and gives himself airs
The hunter does not know
The hunter does not see

    And many times during the week
    He takes the highway to the peak
    Of his entranced Golgotha where
    He can exhale both his own grief
    And at the same time find relief
    For all those others not yet there
    Who in their souls must surely bear
    The scars of silence past belief

    Yes but at Golgotha's base
    Girls and soldiers set a pace
    That is both dear and fast

Their house is one of ill-fame
But they so wrapped in shame
Cannot see the balm
Of the night's calm
That creeps overland at last

Sometimes he reaches his hand
Over the lying page and
Grips a flaming crayon to try
A red-letter writing that sings
The catlike quality of things
The how and why of a world that
Can find no answer but what
to so many questions it brings.

He'll see without notice on his part
It's not on paper that the heart
Of man will ever bleed at all
As it tries to make the bird of song
He'll learn on-high will not belong
with down-low as one
Combination
Entirely in the same symbol

All ends alone on his mountain
His eyes o'erlook from Shippegan
As far as Paris the whole scene
The view from there gives more delight
When garbage cans are not in sight
As in full glow the glossy sheen
Of flower-bed blooms between
The set plum trees that dot the height

In Songs We Love

In songs we love the words disclose
The seed of fear that in us flows
Form out the heart, that leafs each vision
And buds and blossoms in the brain
With spines to prick our calm repose.

O right the first true poet chose
The thorny sweetness of the rose
To live from age to age again
In songs we love.

A rose of death inside us grows,
And that is why we love the rose:
As oysters close their pearls on pain,
Above our sharp-thorned fears again
We feel the crimson flowers close
In songs we love.

As If
After the French of Pierette Le Bel-Saint-Jacques

As if
    it was necessary
    to buckle a belt
    to slope
    to waver
    toward unlimited clarity
Everything
    that lets one suppose
    a false report maybe
    Clearing the way
    through frozen fogs

And
> by its senseless flight
> becoming a dream, resting, or once more my "Eagle"
> that moves

But
> which stops at an orderly light

THE LITTLE CHURCH
After the French of Olivier Mercier Gouin

The little church in fact
Has yielded to the times
Its stones are moss-attacked,
Its beadle is humpbacked,
Its curé's purse is packed,
And through its windows, cracked,
A breeze is humming rhymes.

Poet (from "The Night Of May")
After the French of Alfred de Musset

Would you need, my dear sister,
A kiss bright lip here,
Or but a tear from eyes?
I'd give you them without stress;
From your loves if any bless
your memory in the skies.
I sing you not happiness,
nor glory, nor health's, glad peak;
Alas! Not even duress!
Mouth is guarding its stillness
In order to hear the heart speak.

We Must Play Well
After the French of Jacques Godbout

There are children in the Sahara
Without toys made in the U.S.A.
They make themselves
But since they have no paper nor scissors
And no paints and paste
They take bones
The bones of wild dead camels.

After The Anglo-Saxon Of Beowulf
Assisted by Murray Kinloch

Unferth the thane,   son of Ecglaf,
Sat at the feet   of the king of the Scyldings.
This voyage of Beowulf,   valiant sea-farer,
Jarred all the joy   from his jealous heart,
Greedy of greatness   by any man garnered
Save for his own deeds   under the sky's dome.
And now he rose openly,   showing resentment:

"Are you that Beowulf   who boasted with Breca,
So foolish to vaunt   the skill of your swimming
That vain of your valour   both of you bade
Good-bye to all caution,   cleaving the current
Over the dread deeps   of death-dealing ocean?
Neither friend nor foe   could prevent that faring,
The anxious trip   You two took in the water.
Both of you embraced   the billows in your arms,
Out there threshing with hands   and gliding
    through the waves;
The sea rolled its wave-swell   whipped by winter winds
And there you two   Toiled for seven nights
Weary and powerless in the power of the water.

If his courage lasts   sometimes Fate saves
The determined warrior   not destined to die,
Such was my case   as it turned out.
Nine of the sea-beasts   I slew with my sword.
I have never heard   of a harder fight
Under the arched sky   or in the sea's stream
Waged ever by any   more wretched man;
Weary I won free   from that web of foes.
Finally the foam-race   through the sea carried me
Till I escaped with my life   in the land of the Finns.
Never, O Unferth,   have I heard
Of your doing such deeds   by dint of your sword.
Neither you nor your brother   in any vigorous battle
Wrought such a work   with your red weapons
(But I must not mention   my exploits too much);
You killed your own brother,   closest, of kinsmen
And hell-damned are you now,   however clever you are.
And now, Unferth,   son of Ecglaf,
I tell you the truth, this terrible monster
Had not had heart   for his horrible deeds
To humble your king   in Heorot hall
Were you as a warrior   what you claim for yourself

I in the sea   stronger was than Breca.
More of its malice   than any one man
My body bore   from the wave's buffets.
Boys were we both   all inexperienced
When brash in our boasting,   we bargained together
To put our two lives   against the seas' peril
But we never went back   on the words of our brag.
We held in our hands   the hilts or bare swords
To ward off the whales   that lurk in the waves.
Unable was Breca,   breasting the swell
Though he divided the water   with all his strength
To distance me,   nor would I abandon him.
Then did we two   For the space of five nights
Stay in the sea,   swimming together
Till the cross-currents   created with foam
Drove us unwilling   in different directions.
And the cruel north wind   as night closed in
Over the furious waves   fought us like a foe,
Buffeting fiercely   in the bitter cold.
Then raged around me   the aroused sea-whales
And I would have perished   in their perilous path
Had I not my hauberk,   hard garment of war.

With its hand-woven links   well plated with gold.
It lay on my breast,   Light and snug fitting
And protected me   against my enemies.
Fast-fisted was I   for one fell moment
Gripped in the grasp   of a grisly fiend
Who drew me down   to the deep sea-floor.
Hardly by good hap   did my sword-hand turn,
Letting me drive   deep with deadly sword
Hilting it home   in the monster's maw.
Thus did the dire fray   destroy the sea-beast.
And thus did these loathly creatures   thrust close to me,
But like a brave man   I beat them away.
When I swung my good sword   surely these monsters
Mindful to make   a meal of me
Had no reason then   to relish their feast.
They had gathered for banquet   near the sea bottom
Who shoreward were washed   on the morning tide.
So spoiled were their sides   from thrusts of my sword
They never have hindered   seafarers again.
Grandly the good light   –God's bright sun'
Stood in the east-sky   and the waves sank
Showing the sea-capes   swept by the wing.

Then did Breca the brawny   beat you at swimming.
Clear in the morning   the current carried
The stronger man   out of the sea's swell
Hence to the home   of the Heathoseames.
From there he made his way   to his own land
Where he held in the love   Of his loyal people
A city, a throne,   and a treasure as well.
Thus the brag of Breca,   the son of Beanston,
In all that he said   there was made good.
Though fierce you have fared   in the grim fight,
And sturdy and scatheless have ever survived,
A worse wyrd, I think,   is waiting for you
If you spend a whole night   watching for Grendel."
Thus did Ecgtheow's son   answer the thane:
"Too much you have drunk   and talked about Breca,
And all on his side,   O Unferth, my friend.
But I shall talk now,   tell truth of the matter."

The Crows

After the French of Emile Nelligan

In my heart I saw a flock of crows in flight,
Crowding that inner pen in gloomy bands,
Great crows from peaks renowned in many lands
They flow by in the moon's and torches' light.

Like a circle our graves, a dismal sight,
That has a zebraed-carrion-feast discovered,
In the ice cold of my bones they hovered,
Waving in their beaks shredded hunks of meat.

Now, this prey ripened for these night-devils' yield
Was merely my tattered life where ever still
Vast enemies arrived converging on it,

Pitiless, tearing with great pecks of every bill,
My soul, a carcase strewn on the daily field,
That those old crows will devour bit by bit.

Glooms

After the French of Emile Nelligan

In my heart the thin mists of sadness crossed
And the caws of its hidden crows conjoin;
And I still ponder on that ship gone down,
My twenty years in a starry sea now lost.

Oh, what can I, like a crucifix, put out
Between my fingers that peace so old and dear
Whose voice and music now I never hear
In the mess my groaning life is all about?

With all my soul long thoughts I fain would have,
Beneath the cypress of that corner grave
Where sleep in icy tombs my childhood's charms.

I can no more. I feel funereal arms
Raise me to reality whose torchlit fumes
Embrace at dead of night my own strange glooms.

This Day
After the French of Alain Grandbois

Walls that hold us
The darkness the Unknown
This and that they told us
And gave us dirges for our very own

Joyless   where no hope blooms
Sin is ordained
And burning souls enchained
Where are the bright rooms

What you are what deep within you gnaws
No one knows   you do not know yourself
Blessed revolt   your strongest firmest oath
Nothing can stifle its laws

The sea's dumb waves swelled in a motion
And the world crumbled he said she said
All this is just a futile notion
We are already feloniously dead

Glory of lineage   thirst for life
Cruelty under love's roofs lurking to leap
Walls of the last day mighty and deep
This knot of keys that sets our wits at strife

No no no entry
Walled villa   beware the dog at the gate
What matters our fate
We are tied to Eternity

NOCTURNE
After the French of Robert Pichette

O Lord! How empty this bed is
like the centuries before you
and the eternity after you
there are folds in the bed-clothes
rumpled by your loins
the pillow keeps the hollow of your head
my hands
through habit
through love
still feel for your back
lissome and sleek
solid like a promise
hoping against all hope.

O Lord! How empty this bed is
my breathing encounters neither your neck
nor your too-large child's face
I would be deaf
and blinder than the dark
if there were no mechanical catch
on this dial-clock which once awakened us.

I loved you
there is the empty bed
a basin of hollow hours
where only your memory is asleep
O Lord! How empty this bed is.

WOUNDS
> *After the French of Alma de Chantal*

The harsh crying of gulls
Sometimes opens up a wound
In a too delicate sky

A gash of wounds in day's thigh

Time's Bright Ash And The Small Dust Of Daylight

After the French of Albert Loseau

Time's bright ash and the small dust of daylight
Are afloat in the morning's misty haze;
A shred of sunlight hides its burning rays
Erasing all we see as if by blight.

Time's bright ash and the small dust of daylight
Lift us up like an invisible beam
Where lost in the blue moonlight's charming dream
We blossom once more in our own despite.

Time's bright ash and the small dust of daylight
Are lying in our hearts like rain gone sour;
In fleeting day and in ephemeral hour
How can we be sure hope and love unite?

Time's bright ash and the small dust of daylight
Contain our vows, our song, even our sighs;
With each passing hour a bit of us dies.
Faced with such recurring death, what is sight?

Time's bright ash and the small dust of daylight.

Energism

Between what we see and what would be
A myriad vexing currents flow
But the struggle to ford them and be free
Creates the only life we know.

Song

After the French of Alfred de Musset

I spoke to my heart too feeble for trust:
"Is it not enough to love a mistress,
And don't you think a change that ceaseless
Will bring unhappiness because of lust?"

He answered me: "It is not enough to last.
It is not enough to love a mistress,
And don't you see a change that is ceaseless
Must bring back bitter-sweet the care-worn path?"

I spoke to my heart almost the same day,
"Isn't this enough for so much sadness,
And don't you see a change that is ceaseless
Must run into grief each step on its way."

He answered me: "It's not enough to last,
Nor is it enough for so much sadness,
And don't you see a change that is ceaseless
Must bring back bitter-sweet the care-worn past."

An Old Story

One time when God was hid from sight
Eve sampled a forbidden delight
And, finding it sweet, that young madam
Picked one like it and gave to Adam,
With knowledge plucked from such a tree
Both owned responsibility
And just enough good sense to grace
A fleeting time, a narrow space.

When all went well, quite drunk with power,
They thanked not God at any hour,
But when their strength and wisdom failed
They turned to Him once more and wailed,
Begging Him to use on their behalf
The might that made their own mere chaff,
Provided that the almighty breath
Would chill their enemies to death.

The Robin In The Woods
After the French of Emile Nelligan

We were reading Werther in the deep woods where
Yesterday a robin sang in boughs above,
And I grasped your white hands, spoke to you of love
As I had spoken other times before.

But of my words and tune you took no care,
Dumb to the urging of a frank young man,
Then, rising, you through periwinkles ran
And, deep moved, you called me, crying out
    "Look here!"

What had fallen from green leaves quivering
Was a suffering bird, stricken though young,
That would soon be dead, poor end of the Spring.

And you wept for it, regretting its song.
While I thought, staring at the deep blue sky,
Robin and love had found the same time to die.

Common Denominator

Everything that is under the sun
Is so by the grace of all energy
That subsists wherever its light rays run,
Whatever their age and their scope may be.

Everything that is within the space
Of this, our planet, holds its present form
According to the flux of time and place
Through which its myriad atoms move and swarm.

Everything that is combines today
With every place it finds contiguous
Life acts together as both food and prey
For the beautiful and the hideous.

Only in one thing our world leaves no jar;
What it is depends upon one bright star.

One Of Life's First Allegories

In a kind of attic to a hen house
I crawled up a ladder to find
A roomful of wooden machines
And since there was nothing else
For a very good child to do,
I hauled up an axe and a saw
And I worked hard for days
To re-arrange them.

When my parents discovered
The results of my actions
In that seldom-visited place
They found the machines too altered
To be put back as they had been,
And I was left with the idea
I had done something bad
That never more could be mended.

Meeting
After the French of Gérald LeBlanc

Something that resembles magic
–surrounds us
embraces us
makes our speech too loud
the city is creeping
into our accents
into precise images
memory has overshadowed us.

Suffering Is Not

After the French of Georges Cartier

Suffering is not
Seeing a tree uprooted
Under the might of storms
And like an absent-minded stranger
Watching the enormous twists
Of its giant branches
As the proud, haughty camp
Of its massive trunk
Bends to the ground.

It is casting but one look
Of love and silence
On the first leaf
That slowly becomes undone
Under the first light wind

LIFE

After the French of Marie-Claire Blais

A strange little life opens
In the dust of the morning.
Feral, impatient and eager
It already stirs the shadows....

A woman dropped it there, humbly
Without a cry
Then went away trembling with fatigue
And bleeding,
Her hands joined in her breasts,
She saw the defiant heavens reel.

And prisoner on that day hardly longer than
Other days,
She continued her work in the fields.

An Autumn Conceit

The great composer in the skies
Played this symphony for our eyes
With colour-tones so rich and clear
That even the dullest sight can hear
And echo rhythms as they fall.

In crimson, gold, beach-brown and rose
The leaves proclaim: "Ripeness is all
And loveliness its ideal close."

Roles

I can't remember whether I became
What I was because of what others said,
Or did they pick out a family name
For me to follow in the ways it led?

Was I a boy because men so called me?
Was more because I was susceptible?
Was I from social pressure truly free?
I scarcely noticed when my life went well

And now I find a crisis in my mind....
Do I always have to be what I am told?
Yesterday–it was something less than kind–
I heard a friend say I was growing old.

After A Wasp-Bite

"After a wasp-bite
the sting must be removed,
a matter of great importance,
Use with a fingernail or,
better still, the edge
of a credit card."

Out of infinite wisdom
the CBC more than government
provided choice.

An Impasse

in all the world there is a curse
Inflicts a universal norm:
There is no way that anarchy
Can rest until it finds its form.

L'ENVOI

Last words that I cannot use
yet know that they must come
when my sweet lady, Muse,
bids me her welcome home.

With her, there will be no need
for space-time to go on;
free with perfect faith to feed
only imagination.

Professor

I stood alone. The students sat, close-massed.
I read my notes, prepared some four years back,
And watched out for attention and its lack.
And as I did, with my eyes I harassed
The sluggards and so they heard me, too, at last.
So far so good—I was not satisfied.
The thoughts I mouthed were much too cut and dried.
I despised the role in which I was cast.

It was not so at first when I prepared
My lectures. I meant those then and they seemed
To fit their purpose. I came to realize
Education as a two-way end-shared
Experience where all should play a part.
After that, I cut myself down in size,
Threw my notes away and spoke from my heart.
The result was better than I had dreamed.

Pot-Pourri

On a white page all the words wait in line
Full of forgotten light that makes us find
The last relics of a lover's goldmine,
Poems remain, dried flowers of the mind.

Shadows

After the French of Jean Guy Pilon

Because one day
I wanted to take her as my fate
My dream recreates her patiently
Under a thousand mysterious forms

She is part bird or woman
Her name trembles with the very syllables
That she may become: water-lily
Sea-gull or sweetheart.

As Time Runs Itself

As time runs itself and mile swallows mile
I grow dismayed at how flimsy a grasp
On reality each one of us has.
But where outside all mental existence
Is time anyway? There surely must be
More to it than the machine register
That notifies me of its whereabouts.

The Willow Basket

Silent in my lodging all the evenings fit
And the lampshield is making an amber orbit
Like a willow basket where I sieve apart
Images and words, grain of my unsettled heart.

Your visage is a mottled infinite fountain
Your drowned body is floating somewhere in its train
Of shadows. A thought on the willow basket would
Capture your memory to make my daily food.

To remember who should sit down beside the Stillness
On the side of that Evening and its Absence,
Belated visitors at days of door light move
Who never brought with them the rich-grained loaf
    of love.

The still evening rises, and it goes somewhere,
The cold darkness has come here hiding its hunger.
The hope in the willow basket spills its last sprout
And falls from my hand whenever the lamp goes out.

There Were Two Of Them
After the French of Micheline de Jordy

There were two of them
lengthened in wall-shadow
two trees dry out of hot wax
dead to the flame of a candle

A Sail Has Dreamed...
After the French of Micheline de Jordy

A sail has dreamed the sea's seamy side
the long voyage

Metaphysical

After the French of Raymond Breau

Like a sot on a spree
I heap rhymes together
Or, like a blood-starved tree
Am dead in cold weather.

To those gone now I call
Just to give them a name
So their bodies I pull
From the dust of the time.

Vainly I reach to live
Beer's maniac laughter
At last a tone I give
To life, his sister pure.

In rhyme for all that's there
My words as songs shall go;
Be blonde or red their hair
I'll drink to them also.

The Lament Of Cresseid
After the Middle Scots of Robert Henryson

O sop of sorrow, sunken into care;
O wretched Cresseid destined for despair,
Gone is your Joy and all your Earthly state,
Of all blitheness now you are bereft and bare.
There is no salve can heal you anywhere,
Fell is your fortune and fallen is your fate;
Your bliss is banished as your pain grows great.
Under the Earth, god grant I buried were
Where none of Greece nor yet of Troy might hear.

Where is your Chamber furnished dainty clean?
Your bed with cloth of gold embroidered green,
Hot wine and spice for your entertainment,
Your little bells of gold and silver sheen;
Your luscious Sweetmeats served on platters clean
And spiked with saffron sauce for condiment:
Your garments gay of goodly ornament;
Your pleasant Linen pinned with golden pin:
Your royal renown? —all these from you are rent.

Where is your garden with its grasses gay?
And flowers which Queen Flora in her play
So painted pleasantly upon the plain,
Where you were wont full merrily in May
To walk and take the dew before the day,
And hear the Merle and Mavis sing their strain
While Ladies fair in Carrolling complain,
And see the Royal Knights in their array,
In garments garnished gay in every grain.

Your high honour and your triumphant power
When you were named of Earthly maids the flower
Is all decayed, your luck has altered so.
Your fair estate is turned to darkness dour,
This Leper's Lodge take for your handsome bower,
For your good bed a bunch of straw must do,
And for the Wine and Meat you used to know
Take Mouldy Bread, rough Wine, and Cider sour.
Save Bowl and Clapper you have nothing now.

My clear, sweet voice and courtly carrolling
With which I once with ladies used to sing
Is like a Crow's to caw in raucous bass.
My shapely body, such a lovesome thing
That men have paid with blood to be its king,
Is now deformed; as for this present face,
No lad can look on it with joy or grace.
I speak thus sighing, stung by sorrow's sting,
Firm-lodged among the Leper Folk always.

O Ladies fair of Troy and Greece, attend
My misery, which none may comprehend:
My ill-starred Lot, my infelicity,
My great mischance which no man can amend.
Be warned by Time who hastens on the end,
And in your mind a mirror make of me:
As I am now, mayhap that even ye,
For all your might, may come to that same end,
Or worse than that if any worse may be.

Nought is your fairness but a fading flower,
Nought is your famous honour, laud, and power,
But empty wind that blows through idle ears.
Your rising red to rot returns its dower.
Example take of me, Fate's Paramour,
Who of such things a woeful witness bears,
All Wealth on Earth, away like Wind it veers.
Therefore beware, soon comes the fatal hour:
Fortune's fickle, howe'er she starts and steers.

Last Verse

After the French of Alfred de Musset

For eighteen months now, death is haunting me
From all sides around, ringing in my ear
After eighteen months of sleepless ennui
Everywhere I sense him, see him clear.

The more I argue with my life's poor dearth
The more such instinct becomes part of me
And just when I want to walk on the earth
I feel my heart is stopping suddenly.

My strength is used for struggle and giving
And all things combat until I repose.
And, like a courser broken by living
My dying courage wavers to its close.

LETTER TO A YOUNG POET
After the French of Gerald LeBlanc

There will always be a poem
waiting for the sound of your voice.

Final Song

After the French of Germain Beauchamp

      Let time die and go down in your footsteps
      You are not Elvira Cassandra or Elsa
for them
for her
I made a song of forgetfulness
the husk the view
from the tower's top when summer in your arms
    grew grey
an old season dead
behind your back
      when you lay naked in the grass and autumn
      traced down there under the leaves your
      red-ribbed form

      you had olive breasts and your belly mottled
      with sunlight attracted my hands so much that
      I wanted to cut them off but why repeat what
      exists no more except in the flesh of a new
      caress

time is forgotten wind is forgotten and memory
has lost its pools but why should that which
has never been memorable that living moment be
mute two knitted bodies unknit duration and no
man will ever know more about it than we

summer was your body and your eyes do you
remember grew dim beneath mine ever since
the day or night when I wrote

I tell you plainly that whole past fades away
to the Middle Ages and earlier even than that
I am imagining a silent time

I am imagining

The Young Tarentine
After the French of André Chenier

Weep, sweet Halcyons. Weep, birds most holy,
And to Thetis dear. Weep melancholy.
Go, weep for Myrto, the young Tarentine.
As ship brought her to shores of Catarine.
Now hymeneal songs and flutes unfold
To restore her to her love's threshold.
A watchful key to her marriage day
Inside her cedar-guarded trousseau lay,
Whose beauty yet unpoured whose perfume there
Would add gold incense to her maiden hair.
Alone on the prow, calling on stars, she,
Caught in a lustful wind, failed to break free
And, half-dazed, far from sailors, meets her doom.
She cries, she falls. . Under the waves' boom
On the sea-bottom, the young Tarentine
Collapses her body in the marine
Debris that is in rock hollows by her,
Take pains to hide her from the hungry mire.

Soon, lovely Nereids, by her command
Lift her above their homes of humid sand,
Carry her to the shore and on this tomb
At Cape Zephyr prepare to seal her doom.
Loud and far-off companions complain.
Naiads, Nereids, Dryads, forming a train
Cry out: "Alas! Your loss is all love's pain,
Your wedding dress will not be worn again,
Around your arms gold cords will not be tied,
And to your hair the bride-scent is denied."

Soil

After the French of Guy Ducornet

Eyes planted as if in agony
and open to the sun-rays on the cliff-face
combteeth-shadows

I set aside the shadows
my father died in the springtime

while working at his garden–grass
that was the day of the Pisan Cantos
with my nails I slit the pages

weeping for being from the north and discovering years
and cypresses hills too yellow
And too dry leaps of ashes
strewn with bones and roots

that was a day of the South and its sunshine
the south again–and the sun

which took me away from myself
from one ocean shore to another
though nailed to the same season
with hot tears on my palm
and last evening's book
"it was in just spring"

the docks and the dirty empty harbour
carry away the actuality of that dying year
glances at a lingering lingering mist on a steel wall
a coming back to one soil and one shade

Of All The Words....

Of all the words that destroy decency
And put our false depravity on view
With a pride that itself is blasphemy
Why should any one mention more than two?

Both "Hiroshima" and "Nagasaki"
Torture conscience to a most obscene squeal
In the heart of a heartless century
Only these words and what they mean are real.

O Night Among All Nights
After the French of Maurice Champagne

O night among all nights

You were never so beautiful as now
Receive our bodies that were born of you
Send them a bit of sky
On which to place their feverish brows
Their hearts multiplied like stars
By love
And their flesh gathered like a mighty sun
By innocence
You can leave our feet upon the earth
For warming up the dead again.

After you have made our bed
Go and tell the day
That we no longer need the sun
In this place
let it be thrown into the sea

Men will drink it then despite themselves
But we
Will continue to seed the darkness
For here
Love and its flowers bud beneath the moon.